D0311787

# EXTREME ANIMALS

# REMARKABLE REPTILES

Isabel Thomas

**www.raintreepublishers.co.uk**
Visit our website to find out more information about Raintree books.

**To order:**
☎ Phone 0845 6044371
🖷 Fax +44 (0) 1865 312263
🖳 Email myorders@raintreepublishers.co.uk

Customers from outside the UK please telephone +44 1865 312262

Raintree is an imprint of Capstone Global Library Limited, a company incorporated in England and Wales having its registered office at 7 Pilgrim Street, London, EC4V 6LB – Registered company number: 6695582

Edited by Daniel Nunn, John-Paul Wilkins, and Rebecca Rissman
Designed by Philippa Jenkins
Picture research by Elizabeth Alexander
Production by Victoria Fitzgerald
Originated by Capstone Global Library
Printed and bound in China by CTPS

ISBN 978 1 406 23780 1
16 15 14 13 12
10 9 8 7 6 5 4 3 2 1

**British Library Cataloguing in Publication Data**
Thomas, Isabel
Remarkable reptiles. -- (Extreme animals)
597.9-dc22
A full catalogue record for this book is available from the British Library.

**Acknowledgements**
We would like to thank the following for permission to reproduce photographs: Alamy pp. 10 (© Dmitry Kobeza), 19 (© Scubazoo); Corbis pp. 8 (© Michael & Patricia Fogden), 11 (© Martin Harvey; Gallo Images), 15 (© Dave Watts/Visuals Unlimited); FLPA pp. 12 (Fabio Pupin), 27 (Mark Moffett/Minden Pictures); Getty Images p. 24 (Mark Deeble and Victoria Stone/OSF); Nature Picture Library p. 13 (© Bence Mate); NHPA p. 16 (Stephen Dalton); Photolibrary pp. 5 (Nick Garbutt/OSF), 6 (Gunter Ziesler/Peter Arnold Images), 7 (Berndt Fischer/Age fotostock), 9 (Ed Reschke/Peter Arnold Images), 14 (Raymond Mendez/Animals Animals), 17 (Nick Garbutt/OSF), 18 (Oxford Scientific), 20 (Wolfgang Kaehler/Superstock); Photoshot p. 21 (© NHPA); Shutterstock pp. 4 (© TessarTheTegu), 22 (© Ryan M. Bolton), 23 (© Summer), 25 (© Stanjoman), 26 (© Julian W).

Main cover photograph of chameleon reproduced with permission of Shutterstock (© infografick). Background cover photograph of snake skin pattern reproduced with permission of Shutterstock (© Sergej Razvodovskij).

Every effort has been made to contact copyright holders of material reproduced in this book. Any omissions will be rectified in subsequent printings if notice is given to the publisher.

Some words are shown in bold, **like this**. You can find out what they mean by looking in the glossary.

# Contents

# Extreme reptiles

Think you know everything about reptiles? Think again! Most reptiles have scaly skin, and can't make their own body heat. But the differences between reptiles are what make them **extreme**.

This gecko's weird body shape helps him to hide.

Some reptiles have bizarre bodies. Some behave in weird ways. These features help them to find **mates** or food – or avoid getting eaten themselves!

# Never hug a boa!

Could you swallow a goat in one gulp? This is no problem for a boa. These huge snakes coil around their **prey** and squeeze it until it can't breathe. Like all snakes, they swallow their meal whole.

One large meal will fill a boa up for six months.

# Sneaky snakes

Small snakes make tasty snacks for **predators**. This coral snake does not need to hide from predators. Its bright colours warn that it has a deadly bite.

The hognose snake should win a Best Actor award! If it gets attacked, it pretends to be dead. Its tongue hangs out. It even makes a disgusting smell like a dead animal.

# Killer crocs

**Saltwater** crocodiles are the largest reptiles in the world. They are powerful **predators**. Crocodiles have the strongest bite of any animal. Being caught in a croc's jaws would be a bit like being trapped under a large car.

11

# Experts at escaping

There are more than 4,500 types of lizards. Some have **extreme** tricks to avoid getting eaten. A gecko doesn't panic if a **predator** grabs its tail. It runs away and leaves its tail behind. Then it grows a new one!

new tail

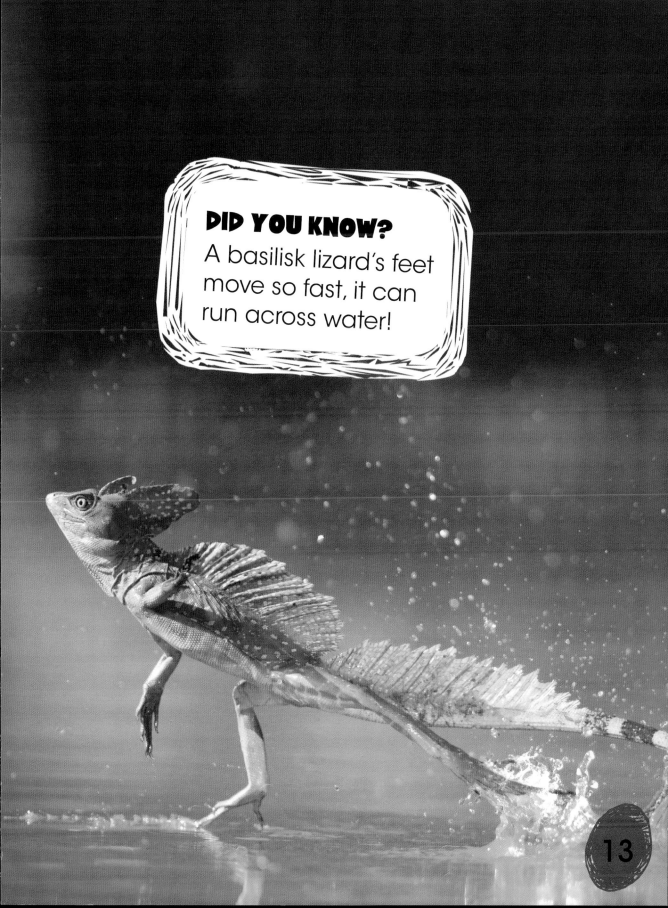

**DID YOU KNOW?**
A basilisk lizard's feet move so fast, it can run across water!

13

Horned lizards **distract** enemies with a disgusting trick. They squirt blood from their eyes! They do this by bursting **blood vessels** around their eyelids. The jet of blood can travel more than one metre.

When an Australian frilled lizard is in danger, it opens its neck frill like an umbrella. This makes it seem bigger.

# Cross-eyed chameleons

Chameleons are famous for changing colour. One of the reasons they do this is to **camouflage**, or hide, themselves.

long, sticky tongue shoots out to grab **prey**

Chameleons have **extreme** eyes. They can point in different directions! They can look out for danger and dinner at the same time.

# Turtle power

When the alligator snapping turtle gets hungry, it sticks its weird tongue out. Fish think that the tongue is a wriggly worm. But it's a trap. When they come to have a nibble, the turtle's jaws go snap!

tongue

**DID YOU KNOW?**
Leatherback turtles can hold their breath for more than one hour.

# Komodo dragons

These fearsome **predators** are the heaviest lizards on Earth. They have jagged teeth like a shark and a **venomous** bite. Komodo dragons knock over big animals and then rip their **prey** to pieces.

venomous
spit

21

# Tough tortoises

Nothing can bite through the shell of a giant tortoise. This helps them to live for more than 100 years. One pet tortoise even lived to celebrate his 255th birthday!

The giant tortoise has a flat nose that helps it to drink through its nostrils. This helps it to suck up water from very shallow pools.

# Awful alligators

Alligators look heavy and clumsy. But these reptiles can spin their bodies like ice skaters. The famous death roll helps alligators to tear **prey** into chunks. They bite their prey and then spin around really fast. They can rip off an arm or a leg in seconds.

powerful
tail

webbed
foot

# Terrible tuataras

Tuataras have three eyes! The third eye can only be seen when they are babies. No one knows what it is for. It may help young tuataras to avoid their parents. Adult tuataras will eat their own babies!

third eye hidden under skin

tail drops off if attacked

**DID YOU KNOW?**
Tuataras have been around since the time of the dinosaurs.

# Record-breakers

Which reptile do you think is the most **extreme**? Why? Have a look at some of these record-breaking reptiles to help you decide.

**What?** Chameleon

**Why?** Longest tongue

**Wow!** Some chameleons have tongues one-and-a-half times as long as their bodies!

**What?** Leatherback turtle

**Why?** World's heaviest reptile

**Wow!** The biggest turtle ever found weighed over 900 kilograms, more than some cars!

**What? Saltwater** crocodile

**Why?** Largest reptile

**Wow!** Males can grow up to 7 metres long, but most are hunted by humans before they get this big.

**What?** Small-scaled snake

**Why?** Most **venomous** snake

**Wow!** These Australian snakes have enough venom to kill 100 adults!

**What?** Spiny-tailed iguana

**Why?** Fastest reptile on land

**Wow!** This reptile from Costa Rica can run at 35 kilometres an hour. That's about the same as a top 100-metre sprinter.

**What?** Dwarf gecko

**Why?** Smallest reptile

**Wow!** Dwarf geckos measure about 16 millimetres from nose to tip of the tail. That's not even as wide as a £1 coin!

# Glossary

**blood vessel** tube in an animal's body that blood moves through

**camouflage** colours or markings that help an animal to blend in with the things around it

**distract** draw somebody's attention away from something

**extreme** unusual, amazing, or different from normal

**mates** two animals that can have baby animals together

**predator** animal that hunts other animals for food

**prey** animal that is hunted by another animal for food

**saltwater** living in salty water

**venomous** able to produce venom. Venomous animals have a poisonous bite or sting.

# Find out more

## Books

*Animal Disguises* (Discover Science), Belinda Weber (Kingfisher, 2011)

*Deadly Reptiles* (Wild Predators), Andrew Solway (Raintree, 2005)

*Killer Snakes* (Animal Attack), Alex Woolf (Franklin Watts, 2011)

*Snakes and Lizards* (Really Weird Animals), Clare Hibbert (Arcturus Publishing, 2011)

## Websites

Watch clips of the world's deadliest reptiles and other animals:
**www.bbc.co.uk/cbbc/shows/deadly-60**

Get face to face with komodo dragons:
**www.bbc.co.uk/nature/life/Komodo_dragon**

Play wild games and read animal books online:
**www.zsl.org/kids/**

# Index